by Susan Albury
illustrated by Mary O'Keefe Young

BOSTON

Printed in China

ISBN 10: 978-0-618-88636-4
ISBN 13: 0-618-88636-2

23456789 SDP 16 15 14 13 12 11 10 09 08

George was curious!
What are all these shapes?

He liked this shape.
He put it on his head.

What shape is George wearing?

Oh no! It was stuck.

Bump-thump! Poor George.

 What shape is the drum?

The drum began to roll. Fast!
It rolled until . . .*ker-plunk*.

What shape is George stuck in now?

George made a mess.
Who helped him out of it?

Cone, cylinder, cube.

George found a favorite shape.

Can you guess what it was?

Responding

Problem Solving

George Shapes Up

Draw Note Important Details

Draw a picture of the shape George liked best.

Tell About

1. Look at page 3.
2. Tell someone what shape George put on his head.

Write

1. Look at page 7.
2. Write the names of the 3 shapes in the story.